DATE DUE			

BUILDING A NATION

NEWCOMERS TO AMERICA
1400's — 1600's

Written by:
Stuart Kallen

NEWCOMERS TO AMERICA

Published by Abdo & Daughters, 6535 Cecilia Circle, Edina, Minnesota 55439

Library bound edition distributed by Rockbottom Books, Pentagon Tower, P.O. Box 36036, Minneapolis, Minnesota 55435

Library of Congress Number: 90-082616   ISBN: 0-939179-86-5

Cover Illustrations by: Marlene Kallen
Inside Photos by: Bettmann Archive
Page 6: Wideworld Photos

Cover Illustrations by: Marlene Kallen
Edited by: Rosemary Wallner

CHAPTER 1
THE VOYAGE THAT CHANGED THE WORLD

The Road to China

Almost 700 years ago in the year 1298, Marco Polo, an Italian merchant, wrote a book called *Description of the World.* In his book, Polo described the 24 years he had spent exploring India, Japan and China. Polo told of huge palaces, silk clothes and streets paved with gold. Polo brought ivory, jade, spices and other treasures from Asia and sold them in Europe for large sums of money.

When people in Europe read Polo's book, they too wanted to explore the exotic markets of Asia. But the road from Europe to Asia was very dangerous. The continents were separated by huge mountains, vast deserts and fierce bandits. By the 1400's people began to seek a water route from Europe to Asia.

The World Is Round!

When Christopher Columbus was a young man he read and reread Marco Polo's book about Asia. Columbus was an expert sailor and he had a revolutionary idea. The world was round! Up until that time most people believed that the world was flat and, if you sailed too far, you would fall off!

Columbus studied his maps over and over and decided that to get to the East he would sail west across the Atlantic Ocean. Sailors from the country of Portugal were trying to reach Asia by sailing south, around the continent of Africa. That was a long and dangerous journey and, so far, no one had reached Asia that way. Columbus' idea became known as the *Northwest Passage* to Asia, and for the next 200 years, hundreds of men would spend their time looking for the fabled Northwest Passage. Today we know that it doesn't exist.

The Daring Vikings

While Columbus dreamt of sailing westward across the Atlantic, he was unaware that the journey had been made by people over 700 years before!

The people that lived in what is now Norway and Sweden called themselves *Vikings*. The Vikings had built settlements on Iceland in the 800's. Eric the Red had sailed to Greenland in the 900's and soon there were Viking villages established there.

Then in the 1000's, Eric the Red's son, Leif Erickson, sailed west of Greenland to a land of dense forests and white sand beaches. Today we know that Leif Erickson had reached Canada. Because of the twisted grape vines growing on the shores, Leif named his discovery *Vinland*. The several villages that the Vikings built disappeared without a trace. Today, Vinland lives on only in legends.

Christopher Columbus.

Columbus Sets Sail

Columbus tried to convince the kings of Portugal, England and France to pay for his trip west. All three refused. They said that the world was much larger than Columbus thought and that he would never reach Asia by sailing west. After several years, Columbus convinced Spain's Queen Isabella and King Ferdinand to fund his expedition. The king and queen knew that if Columbus discovered a water route to Asia it would bring great riches to Spain.

In August of 1492, Christopher Columbus set sail in three ships, the *Nina, Pinta* and *Santa Maria*. Each ship was 100 feet long and carried thirty sailors.

Columbus Discovers a New World

Once upon a time, there was a tribe of people who called themselves the Arawaks. They lived on an island they called Guanahani, now known as the Bahamas. The Arawaks grew corn and yams and were expert weavers. They lived in

Santa Maria   Pinta   Nina

giant bell-shaped houses made of strong wood and roofed with palm leaves. Their huge log houses could hold several hundred people. The Arawaks decorated themselves with feathers, bone jewelry and colored stones. They lived free and easy, gladly trading their possessions with each other and sharing in the world and the food.

One warm morning on October 12, 1492, there was great excitement among the Arawak men and women. Three huge ships were floating in the crystal blue waters that surrounded their island paradise!

Land at Last

After three tough months at sea, Columbus and his sailors had finally reached land. Columbus had been lying to his sailors, afraid to tell them how far they had journeyed into the unknown. The sailors had been begging their captain to turn around for weeks, but Columbus had refused.

When Columbus spotted the sandy beaches, he thought he had reached the islands near Asia known as the Indies. In fact, he had landed on an island in what is known as the Bahamas. When Columbus met the Arawak people who lived on the island, he mistakenly called them Indians.

In the year 1492, there were already several million people in 600 different tribes living in North and South America. Because of Columbus' mistake, the Native Americans came to be called Indians.

A Friendly People

When Columbus and his sword carrying sailors came ashore, the Arawaks ran to greet them with food, water and gifts. They were a very friendly and unselfish tribe. Columbus later wrote in his journal:

"They brought us parrots and balls of cotton and spears and many other things, which they exchanged for glass beads and bells. They willingly traded every thing they owned . . . They were well built with handsome features . . . They do not bear arms and cut themselves on our swords out of ignorance. They have no iron. They would make fine servants. I took several of them by force so that they might give me information."

The information that Columbus wanted the most was: where could he find gold?

The Search for Treasures

For the next three months, Columbus searched in vain for gold, jewels and other riches. He found traces of gold in the streams but no vast gold fields. What Columbus and his Arawak guides did find were the islands of Hispaniola and Cuba. When the *Santa Maria* ran aground on Hispaniola, Columbus and his men built a fort out of the ships timbers. He called the fort *Navidad* (which means "Christmas" in Spanish) and left 39 sailors there. Navidad was the first Spanish settlement on the western side of the Atlantic.

Columbus returned to Spain a hero. The king and queen named him "Admiral of the Ocean Sea, Viceroy and Governor of the Islands that he had discovered in the Indies."

Columbus Returns Again and Again

Christopher Columbus was sure that he had discovered the water route to Asia. He thought that he had come close to the Asian continent. But what he did not know was that the huge landmass of North and South America and the Pacific Ocean lay between Europe and Asia.

Columbus convinced the Spanish king and queen to fund another expedition. He thought that this time he would sail past the islands to Asia. On September 25, 1493, Columbus left Spain with 17 ships and 1,500 men.

When Columbus reached the island of Hispaniola, he found no sign of the fort and the men that he had left behind. Columbus and his sailors enslaved the Arawak Indians and put them to work growing food and digging for gold.

Columbus returned to Spain in 1496. He was very disappointed that he had not found China. In 1498, Columbus made another voyage across the Atlantic. This time he brought men, women, plants, seed, farm animals and tools. The travelers started a new life in South America, but still, Columbus found no gold.

When Columbus returned to Spain in 1498, he was told that Vasco da Gama, a Portuguese explorer had reached Asia by sailing around Africa. The news made Columbus even more desperate to find the western route to Asia.

In 1502, Columbus made his final voyage across the Atlantic Ocean. He sailed into every river, inlet and bay trying to find a waterway to Asia. Defeated, Columbus returned to Spain. In 1506, he died a poor and unhappy man. He never knew that he had discovered the richest continent in the world.

And They Called It "America"

Barrels. Muskets. Plants. Food. Gunpowder. The list of goods that Columbus needed for his journeys was long and expensive. The man who sold those important supplies was Amerigo Vespucci, an Italian merchant living in Spain. After hearing Columbus' extraordinary tales, he decided Columbus had not reached Asia at all. Vespucci traveled across the Atlantic and studied the land and the forest of the New World.

Amerigo Vespucci.

Many of the plants and animals Vespucci saw were unknown in Europe and Asia. Vespucci was certain that Columbus had discovered a new continent.

A German mapmaker read some articles about the new continent that Vespucci had written. When he made a map of the new continent, he named it *America* in honor of Amerigo Vespucci. When the Europeans discovered there were two continents, they called them North America and South America.

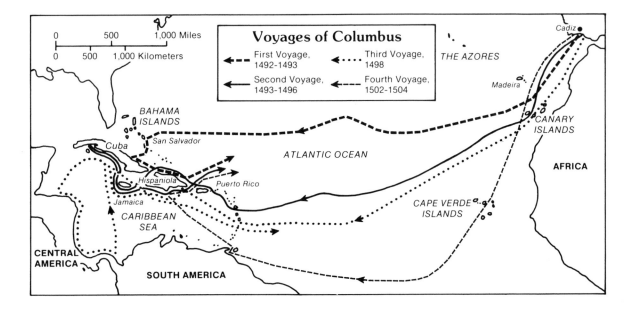

Voyages of Columbus

First Voyage, 1492-1493
Second Voyage, 1493-1496
Third Voyage, 1498
Fourth Voyage, 1502-1504

CHAPTER 2
THE SPANISH EXPLORERS

A Land of Riches

Iron ore! Huge rivers teeming with fish! Vast forests full of hardwood trees! Furs! Delicious foods, like corn, that were unknown to Europe! And yes, even gold and other precious metals. When Columbus died, he had no idea that his discovery would forever change the way that Europeans lived, ate and survived. It would also change forever the lives of the Native Americans that lived in the New World as millions were wiped out by the land hungry Europeans.

By the 1500's Europe was a crowded place with few opportunities for many of the people that lived there. Many countries were quickly running out of food, energy and land. The Americas, whose size was four times greater than Europe, seemed to be the solution to their problems.

De Soto Starts a New Adventure

Hernando de Soto was a very rich man. He had fought with Juan Pizzaro in Peru, where they had destroyed the beautiful cities that were built by the Inca Indians. The Inca's cities were filled with gold, silver and jewels. After slaughtering the Incas, Pizzaro and his men had stolen as much gold as they could carry. The Spaniards had taken over the Inca cities and had loaded ships full of gold to be sent to Spain. De Soto was one of the men who had gained great wealth at the expense of the Incas.

However, de Soto was not happy to live the life of a rich man. He wanted more adventure. In May 1539, de Soto and 600 soldiers landed in what is now Tampa Bay, Florida. On a search for more cities of gold, de Soto started cutting through the swamps of present-day Florida.

On to the Mississippi River

Dressed in armor and carrying heavy weapons, de Soto's men marched through forests and crossed rivers. Their journey took them through what is now South Carolina, Georgia, Alabama and Tennessee. But de Soto's luck was running out. Nearly half his men had died from fever or had been killed fighting with the Indians.

De Soto's discovery of the Mississippi River.

18

For the next two years de Soto and his men battled fierce Indians. His problems were multiplied by the poisonous snakes and mosquitos in the dense tangled forests. In April 1541, the weary soldiers reached the Mississippi River.

De Soto was not pleased that he had found one of the longest and most beautiful rivers in the world. He wanted gold. He led his men along the banks of the river and up to the Arkansas River. De Soto traveled as far as present-day Oklahoma before giving up. In 1542, he died of fever along the banks of the Mississippi.

De Soto's explorations gave Spain a claim to huge portions of land in southern and eastern North America.

Coronado's Journey

While de Soto slogged his way through the swamps of Florida, another Spaniard was searching for gold in the Southwest. Francisco Coronado had an easier time leading his men through Arizona and New Mexico. The Zuni and Pueblo Native American tribes were friendly. One of Coronado's men was the first European to see the Grand Canyon. Coronado led his men as far as present-day Kansas where huge herds of buffalo roamed the plains.

Francisco Coronado.

Coronado returned to Mexico without finding any gold, but his journey gave Spain a claim to huge portions of the southwestern part of North America. Although that part of the country was rich in gold and silver, Coronado could not find it. The gold lay in rich veins buried deep in the ground.

CHAPTER 3
THE ENGLISH COME TO AMERICA

Powerful Spain

By the middle of the 1500's, Spain had become the richest nation in Europe. Her ships controlled the New World. The gold stolen from the Incas in Peru had made her very rich. Spain's riches made her the envy of other European countries. Soon the other countries were sending explorers to the New World.

At first, the English had no plans for the New World. They just wanted to find as much gold and silver as possible and discover the fastest sea route to Asia.

 Yᵉ Ideal Pirate

Pirates, also known as Sea Dogs, attacked ships.

Sea Dogs

Great tensions developed between England and Spain over who would control the Atlantic Ocean. Slowly, an undeclared war developed between the two countries. Into the middle of this war stepped the sea dogs. Eager for riches, but also loyal to England, the sea dogs were pirates who captured Spanish gold ships and gave part of the ship's treasures to the English government. The sea dogs were also slave traders. They captured the African people and made them work as slaves in the New World.

One of the most daring sea dogs was Sir Francis Drake. In 1573, Drake captured the annual silver shipment bound for Spain. He then sailed down the coast of South America and stole from the Spanish settlements. In 1580, Drake returned to England with millions of dollars worth of gold, silver and jewels.

In 1588, Spain sent her war ships to fight the English. When Spain lost, the English gained control of the Atlantic.

Sir Francis Drake.

The Colony at Roanoke

In 1585, Sir Walter Raleigh spent much of his personal fortune to start the first English colony in America. He loaded seven ships with 100 men, women and children. They sailed to Roanoke Island off the coast of what is today North Carolina.

Within a year, the unhappy settlers returned to England. In 1587, Raleigh tried again. This time he brought 117 people. Later that year their captain, John White, returned to England, leaving behind a thriving colony as well has his granddaughter, Virginia Dare. Virginia was the first English child born in America.

The Lost Colony

Because of England's war with Spain, White did not return to Roanoke until three years later. When he did return, White found deserted buildings, rusty armor and weeds growing in the paths. All the people were gone. The word *CROATOAN* was carved in the post of a crumbling fort. That was the name of the Indian tribe in the area. A storm prevented White from searching for his friends and family.

Did the settlers run off to join the Indians? Were they massacred? To this day no one knows what happened to the missing colony of Roanoke Island.

The Jamestown Colony

Settling a colony in an untamed wilderness thousands of miles from England was a risky business. In England, wealthy people pooled their money to form companies known as *joint-stock companies*. The joint-stock companies gave people the supplies and ships they needed to settle colonies in America. If the colonies were successful, the profits would go to the owners of the company.

In December 1606, the London Company sent 144 men and boys on three small ships to start a colony in Virginia. The voyage was long and hard, but in April 1607, the ships entered Chesapeake Bay. They sailed 30 miles up the James River to a small stretch of land surrounded on three sides by water. To the tired travelers, the area looked like a great place to set up a colony.

The bushes were thick with wild strawberries and the woods were full of deer, beaver and other animals. The men left their ships and built a colony that they called Jamestown after the King of England, James I.

Starving in a Land of Plenty

The settlers had made a poor choice when they built Jamestown. The land was swampy and when summer came, mosquitos and other insects spread disease and fever. Within six months, half of the settlers had died.

To add to their troubles, the food they had brought with them was gone within six months. Since most of the settlers were from the city, they did not know how to hunt or fish. They began to starve even though there were plenty of fish in the river and many animals in the woods. To make matters worse, the London Company demanded that the settlers search for gold. With everyone looking for gold, no one had time to plant crops.

John Smith Steps In

The London Company appointed 13 men to govern Jamestown. There was so much disagreement among the governors that they did nothing to help the starving settlers. Finally, a man named John Smith took over the council.

Smith ordered the men to clear land and plant crops. He also stopped the hunt for gold that had wasted everyone's energy. Smith traded with the Algonquin Indians to get food for Jamestown.

The Algonquins, however, were unhappy with the white men clearing their land. They kidnapped Smith and threatened to kill him. The chief's daughter Pocahontas begged for Smith's life and he was released. Afterwards, Pocahontas secretly brought food to the starving Englishmen.

New Hope for Jamestown

In 1609, John Smith returned to England. That winter, the cold weather, disease and fights with the Indians killed many of the settlers. By spring, the remaining 60 men decided to go back to England. As they were sailing down the James River to leave, they were greeted by two ships carrying 300 new settlers. The settlers had supplies, tools and a new leader, Lord Delaware.

Delaware ordered the men back to Jamestown. He had plans for a cash crop that would bring great profit to the failing colony.

After Lord Delaware came to Jamestown, a farmer named John Rolfe arrived. Rolfe had seen the Spanish making a lot of money growing a plant called tobacco. Tobacco grew wild in America and the Indians had been smoking it for centuries. Tobacco smoking had caught on in Europe and there was a great demand for it. Rolfe knew that the climate in Virginia was perfect for growing tobacco. Within a few years, everyone in Jamestown was growing it.

Bringing tobacco to market.

Orphans, Wives and Convicts

Even wth the profits from tobacco, the London Company was having a hard time finding people to move to Jamestown. By 1617, over 2,000 people had traveled to Jamestown, but only 400 had survived.

In the late 1600's, London Company workers kidnapped 100 orphans and sent them to Jamestown. If a man committed a crime in England, he was sent to Jamestown instead of jail. In 1620 and 1621 the company brought groups of unmarried women to start families in Jamestown.

Tobacco and Slavery

Tobacco guaranteed the survival of Jamestown. But it helped start a sad chapter in American history.

Growing tobacco involved a lot of backbreaking labor. The settlers of Jamestown were not used to that kind of work.

In 1619, a ship with 20 Africans arrived at Jamestown. The Africans were sold as slaves to the tobacco growers. At first, the Africans worked side by side in the fields with the English. But by 1670, things had changed. Slavery had become a fact of life in the Virginia colony.

Slaves being traded at market.

The Pilgrims

When most people think of the first settlers in America they think of the Pilgrims. But the Pilgrims did not arrive in America until 1620. By that time, Jamestown was a thriving colony.

The Pilgrims were a religious group in England. Because their views differed from the official Church of England, they were not allowed to worship freely. The Pilgrims left England and went to the Netherlands to practice their form of Christianity.

But the Pilgrims were not happy in the Netherlands. In September 1620, 102 men, women and children left Plymouth, England, aboard a small ship called the *Mayflower*. Their destination was Jamestown.

The Plymouth Colony

On November 9, the Pilgrims landed on the sandy beach of Cape Cod in what is now Massachusetts. High winds and storms had blown their tiny ship hundreds of miles off course. Snow covered the ground and winter held its icy grip on the seas. The Pilgrims decided it was too late in the year to return to England or to sail south to Jamestown. They decided to set up a colony where they had landed.

Before leaving the ship, the Pilgrims drew up a document called the Mayflower Compact. This document set up the first government of the colonies. The Mayflower Compact stated that the government had a right to make laws for the good of all. The 41 men on the ship signed the agreement and chose John Carver to be their governor.

Native American Friends

The Pilgrims named their new colony *Plymouth*. The area they had chosen had a good harbor. The land had been cleared by the Indians who lived in the area.

But in spite of the good location, the first winter was harsh for the Pilgrims. Over half of them died, including John Carver. The Pilgrims stubbornly refused to return to England. They elected a new governor, William Bradford, and stayed through the winter. Later, Bradford wrote a book titled *History of the Plimoth Plantation*. In his book, Bradford described the Pilgrims' early years in Plymouth.

One day in March 1621, a Native American man walked into Plymouth and greeted Bradford in English. His name was Samoset. He had learned to speak English from the fishermen that had passed through his area. Samoset said, "Much welcome Englishmen! Much welcome!" Samoset introduced the Pilgrims to Squanto, another Native American who spoke English.

Squanto taught the Pilgrims many survival skills. From Squanto the Pilgrims learned how to rake clams at low tide and tap maple trees for maple syrup. Squanto also showed the Pilgrims how to grow corn, a grain they had never seen before. The friendly Native Americans also showed the Pilgrims which wild plants they could eat and how to hunt deer and beaver. Because of these friendly people, the Pilgrims and their colony thrived.

The First Thanksgiving

By the fall of 1621, the Pilgrims had worked hard and had plenty of food to get them through the winter. Because the Pilgrims were grateful, they decided to have a celebration to give thanks to God for their good fortune. The Pilgrims invited their Native American friends to join their feast.

For three days the Pilgrims and 90 Native Americans feasted on lobsters, clams, wild turkey, duck, geese, cornbread, fruit and cranberries. They counted their blessings and gave thanks to God for their food, their friends and their new colony. This is where the American holiday of Thanksgiving originated.

The Puritans

While the Pilgrims were building a colony in Plymouth, another religious group was building a colony north of them in Boston. The Puritans had tried to change the Church of England and were driven out of that country by the angry king.

In 1630, over 1,000 Puritans arrived in Boston and set up the Massachusetts Bay Company. By 1643, over 20,000 people had come to Boston and the surrounding area. By 1691, the Puritans and the Pilgrims united in one colony called Massachusetts.

Maryland

The Catholics were another group of people who were not allowed to practice their religion in the Protestant country of England. They, too, came to America to avoid English prejudice.

In 1634, Sir George Calvert started a colony and named it Maryland, after Queen Mary of England. His son, Cecilius Calvert encouraged people of any religion to settle in Maryland. He promised that they could worship as they pleased.

The people of Virginia showed the new colonies how to grow tobacco. Soon England had three thriving colonies in America: Virginia, Massachusetts and Maryland.

Sir George Calvert, founder of Maryland.

CHAPTER 4
THE FRENCH COME TO AMERICA

Land of Fish and Fur

Like other European countries, France was excited by the new land called America. In 1524, the French hired Giovanni da Verrazano to explore North America. Verrazano sailed from what is now North Carolina all the way to Newfoundland in present-day Canada. Like others before him, he found the seas teeming with fish and the forests full of valuable furbearing animals. And like the others before him, he failed to find a water route to Asia.

Verrazano's tales of the New World excited many Frenchmen. Soon French fishermen were harvesting the seas of America for their hungry countrymen. But the French were having political and religious strife at home, and the French exploration of the New World was limited until the 1600's.

In 1610, Frenchman Samuel de Champlain, a mapmaker, explored and mapped the Great Lakes region. He traveled north through Lake Ontario and Lake Huron.

The Priest and the Fur Trapper

The French spent the 1600's establishing colonies around the Great Lakes in what is now Canada. French fur trappers made plenty of money exporting beaver furs to France, where beaver hats were a popular fashion. The French fur trappers worked closely with the Native Americans and trapped thousands of beaver until there were almost none left.

In the spring of 1673, Jacques Marquette, a priest, and Louis Joliet, a fur trapper, traveled through North America. The two men were from Quebec, Canada. From the Native Americans they had heard about a great river to the west. They thought that the river might lead to Asia.

The Mighty Mississippi River

Joliet, Marquette and five other men paddled their canoes through the clear, cold waters of Lake Michigan. Day after day they paddled until they reached present-day Green Bay, Wisconsin. They pulled their canoes from the water and carried them across land for miles and miles.

Father Marquette approaches the Indians with a peace pipe.

The explorers finally reached the banks of the Wisconsin River. They returned their canoes to the water and paddled south until they reached the mighty Mississippi River.

Marquette and Joliet continued down the Mississippi for hundreds of miles until they reached the Arkansas River. There, they were told by the Native Americans that the Mississippi flowed south, not west. Once again, a group of explorers failed to find the fabled Northwest Passage to Asia. The men returned to Quebec.

New France

In 1682, Robert de La Salle, another French explorer, retraced Marquette and Joliet's journey. La Salle sailed all the way down the Mississippi River to the Gulf of Mexico. When he reached the gulf, La Salle planted a cross on the shore and claimed all the land from the Great Lakes to the Gulf of Mexico for France. He called this vast area New France. The area La Salle claimed for France was two-thirds of North America. By the late 1700's, only 100,000 French people lived in New France.

Robert de La Salle claiming all the land from the Great Lakes to the Gulf of Mexico for France.

CHAPTER 5
THE DUTCH IN AMERICA

The Dutch Start a Colony

In the 1600's the Netherlands was one of the richest countries in Europe. The Dutch had been trading in Asia for years and had gotten rich on the spices, jewels and silks of the Orient. But the trip around Africa to Asia was long and costly. In 1609, a group of Dutch merchants hired an Englishman named Henry Hudson to find the Northwest Passage to Asia.

Hudson reached America in the fall of 1609 and steered his ship, the *Half Moon* up a long, deep river. Hudson thought he had found the passage. But as he sailed, the river got narrower and more shallow. Hudson sailed to what is present-day Albany, New York. Disappointed, Hudson returned to the Netherlands. Today the river he sailed on is known as the Hudson River.

While Hudson and his men explored New York, they traded with the Native Americans who lived along the banks of the river. When they returned to the Netherlands, there was much excitement over the furs that they had brought back. Soon, Dutch ships were sailing to America and returning home stuffed with furs.

In 1624, the king of the Netherlands gave the Dutch West India Company the right to settle and trade along the Hudson River and in what is now New Jersey and Connecticut. The company sent thirty families to America. The families were told to spread out and claim as much land as possible. When they arrived they began to build trading posts along the Hudson and Delaware rivers.

The English Capture New Amsterdam

The Dutch West India Company governed the new Dutch colonies. But the settlers that lived in these colonies were unhappy because the company made strict rules and taxed their income. The Algonquin Indians who traded with the company felt that they were getting cheated. Many colonists broke the laws. Soon New Amsterdam was full of smugglers and pirates. Fighting broke out with the Algonquins.

Trouble was also brewing with the English who wanted control of the harbor and trade in New Amsterdam. In 1664, the English sent 4 ships and 900 soldiers to take over the Dutch colony. The people in New Amsterdam gave up without a fight because they did not like the strict rules that the Dutch imposed on them. When the Dutch surrendered their colony, New Amsterdam was renamed New York after the King of England's brother.

A Final Word

The first two hundred years after the European discovery of America were hard years for the people that carved settlements out of the wilderness. Hunger and disease were everyday facts of life for the early settlers. All the work was done by hand. All travel was done by foot, by horse or by boat. The early settlers faced hardships that a modern person could barely imagine. Also, the Native Americans suffered greatly when their lands and people were destroyed by the Europeans.

But this is the rich history of one of the greatest countries on the earth. The discovery of America and her rise to power is unlike the story of any other country. When we know our history and where we come from, it may give us an idea of where we are going.

INDEX